BOUDICA

Written by Claire Llewellyn
Illustrated by Laura Tolton

CONTENTS

WHO WAS BOUDICA?

Boudica was a queen who lived in Britain about 2,000 years ago. Britain was very different then. It was home to many **tribes**, who lived in different parts of the country. Boudica was queen of a tribe called the Iceni.

In about 43 CE, when Boudica was a young girl, Britain was invaded by the Romans. From then on, the Romans controlled all the tribes, and took their land and money.

About 20 years after the invasion, Boudica rose up against the Romans. She built an army, raided Roman towns and led her warriors into battle.

This book is all about Boudica. It explains why
and how she fought the Romans and why she's still
remembered today.

DID YOU KNOW?

The name Boudica means "victory".
The name is written and said
in various ways: as Boudica,
Boudicca and Boadicea.

WHO WERE THE ROMANS?

The Romans were a tough and powerful people, who came from Rome in Italy. They built a strong army with bold commanders and well-trained soldiers, who were well armed.

From about 200 BCE, the Romans used their army to conquer other lands. In just a few hundred years, they built a huge **empire**, which was ruled over by an emperor. The people they conquered had to learn a new language, follow Roman laws and pay high **taxes**. The taxes made Rome rich. The money helped to pay for the army and build roads and towns.

In about 58 BCE, the Romans invaded **Gaul**. Britain lay just over the sea, so the Romans decided to invade it too.

Britain

France
(Gaul)

Spain

Italy

Rome

North Africa

Middle East

the purple areas show the Roman Empire in 41 CE

a modern reconstruction showing Roman
soldiers lined up ready for battle

5

WHAT WAS BRITAIN LIKE BEFORE THE ROMANS?

At this time, the people of Britain weren't a single nation. Instead, there were lots of different tribes, who spoke similar languages and could understand one another.

Each tribe lived in a particular region, and had its own king or queen. Boudica's tribe, the Iceni, lived in what's now Norfolk. Tribes sometimes fell out with their neighbours and fought one another.

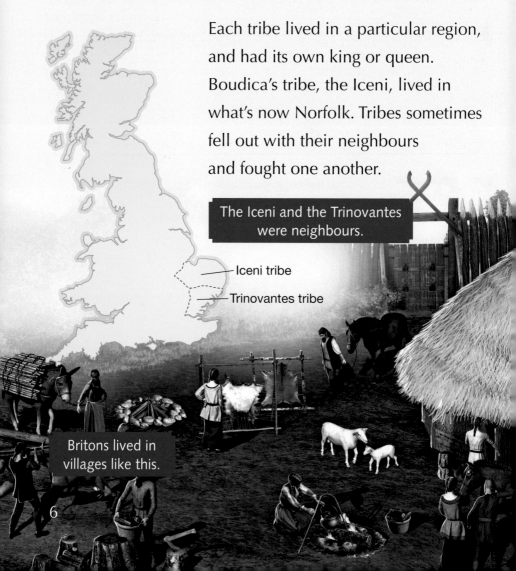

The Iceni and the Trinovantes were neighbours.

Iceni tribe

Trinovantes tribe

Britons lived in villages like this.

Most people had small farms and lived a simple, country life. There were no roads, no fine buildings and no large towns, so it was all very different from Rome.

To the Romans, the Britons seemed rough and uncivilised. In fact, they were skilled artists who made beautiful metal goods, such as shields, brooches, coins and pots.

These beautiful pieces of ancient British metalwork were found in the River Thames.

DID YOU KNOW?
The Roman name for Britain was Britannia.

7

A CLOSER LOOK: LIFE IN BRITAIN BEFORE THE ROMANS

ROUND HOUSES

Britons lived in small round houses built of wood, straw and mud. The houses had thick thatched roofs and no windows.

wall

hill

ditch

HILLFORTS

Hillforts were larger villages built on top of hills. People dug deep ditches around their village so they could defend it from enemy tribes.

CLOTHES

Clothes were made from **linen** or wool. Men wore tunics, trousers and cloaks, while women wore dresses, skirts and shawls. Clothes were coloured using dyes made from berries and plants.

JEWELLERY

People loved jewellery.
They fastened their
cloaks with
brooches and
pins made from
bronze, tin,
silver or gold.
The rich wore metal
neckbands called "torcs".

a solid gold torc

FOOD

People gathered or grew food,
such as grains, vegetables, berries
and nuts. They hunted deer and
other wild animals, and they kept
cows, chickens, goats and sheep.

9

WHEN DID THE ROMANS INVADE BRITAIN?

The famous general Julius Caesar invaded Britain in 55 BCE. However, bad weather and fierce fighting by the Britons caused him great problems, and he returned to Gaul.

About 100 years later, in 43 CE, there was a new Roman emperor called Claudius. He wanted more land, more money and more glory for Rome. He also wanted to show he was a great commander, so he decided to invade Britain again.

DID YOU KNOW?

Britain was about 2,000 kilometres from Rome. Many Romans believed that it lay at the very edge of the world.

A huge army of
40,000 soldiers
landed on the south
coast of Britain.
They marched inland,
attacking hillforts until
the locals surrendered.
Then they pushed on
further north and defeated
more and more tribes.

This time the Roman invasion
succeeded, and life in Britain
changed for ever.

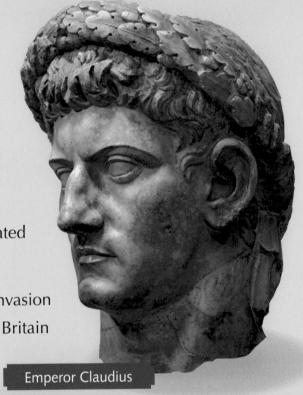

Emperor Claudius

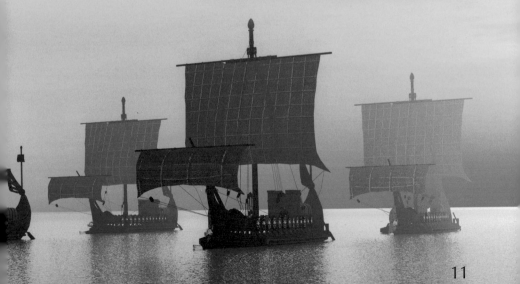

WHAT HAPPENED AFTER THE INVASION?

Over the next 20 years, the Romans put down roots in Britain. They built forts to defend themselves, and towns where their soldiers could live. In the south-east of England, the towns of Colchester, London and St Albans all became important.

The Romans built good roads, which made it easier for people to travel and buy and sell their goods. **Trade** and wealth began to grow.

This Roman road at Blackstone Edge, Greater Manchester, is still visible today.

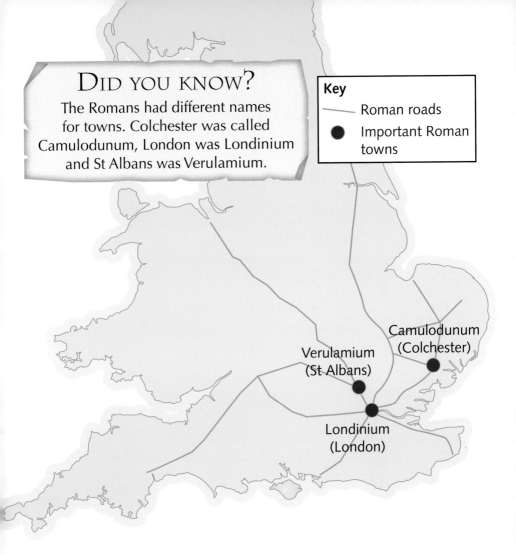

Key

— Roman roads
● Important Roman
  towns

Verulamium
(St Albans)

Camulodunum
(Colchester)

Londinium
(London)

Colchester became the capital city. It was a place where
older soldiers lived when they retired from the army.
A big stone temple was built in the town, and dedicated
to Emperor Claudius. The local people hated the temple;
they had different beliefs.

HOW DID THE INVASION AFFECT LOCAL PEOPLE?

Some tribes suffered greatly after the Roman invasion. One tribe, called the Trinovantes, lived in what's now Essex. When the Romans marched into Colchester, the Trinovantes lost their most important town.

The Trinovantes lost their land, too, and were forced to work in the fields like slaves. They also had to pay high taxes, so they had good reason to hate the Romans.

Boudica and her husband Prasutagus were the wealthy rulers of the Iceni, a tribe that lived close to the Trinovantes. In 47 CE, they decided to work with the Romans rather than oppose them. In return, the Romans allowed Prasutagus and Boudica to remain as rulers of the Iceni. The tribe were charged lower taxes, and were allowed to keep their land.

Boudica and Prasutagus agreeing a deal with a Roman official

WHAT DO WE KNOW ABOUT BOUDICA?

Boudica was born around 25 CE, but we know very little about her. There are no pictures of the queen. All we have is a description of her by a Greek historian called Cassius Dio, who wrote about Boudica long after she'd died.

He described her as a tall woman with long, tawny hair.
She had a harsh voice and steely eyes, and wore a colourful
tunic, a gold neckband and a thick cloak pinned with
a brooch. Is this a true picture? We just don't know.

Boudica and Prasutagus had two young daughters.
The family enjoyed a comfortable life until Prasutagus died.
Then things turned very bad indeed.

WHAT HAPPENED AFTER PRASUTAGUS DIED?

King Prasutagus died in about 59 CE. Before his death, he made a will leaving half of his land and fortune to the Romans and half to his daughters. He hoped his will would protect his family and avoid trouble with the Romans.

Sadly, Prasutagus was mistaken. Roman **officials** ignored his will. They sent in soldiers to plunder his home and his lands. They helped themselves to everything he'd left behind.

Queen Boudica protested angrily. How dare the Romans treat her family like this? How dare they rob her of her wealth and land? Her protests only made matters worse.

18

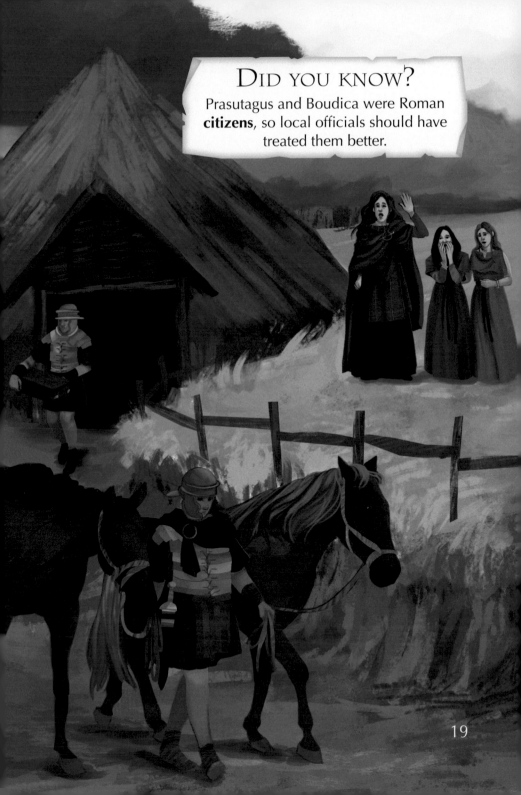

DID YOU KNOW?

Prasutagus and Boudica were Roman **citizens**, so local officials should have treated them better.

WHAT DID THE ROMANS DO TO BOUDICA?

The Roman officials decided to teach Boudica a lesson. They whipped the queen in public. They hurt her daughters in front of her eyes. They also punished Iceni nobles: they took their land, turned them into slaves and ordered them to give up their weapons.

In a few short days, everything had changed. Boudica had been a friend of the Romans; now she was their worst enemy. She, her daughters and her tribe had been robbed, attacked and shamed. She'd make the Romans pay for this! Never would the Iceni be Roman slaves!

Boudica began to dream of revenge. Revenge was dangerous, of course, but what more did she have to lose?

WHO MIGHT HAVE STOPPED BOUDICA?

One person might have stopped Boudica in her plans for revenge. He was the Roman governor of Britain, a man called Suetonius Paulinus. Paulinus governed Britain with a firm hand. He dealt harshly with anyone who resisted Roman rule.

Around the time that Prasutagus died, there was trouble in north Wales. Local priests called Druids were urging people to stand up to the Romans. Paulinus wanted to stamp out the Druids so he marched to Wales with 10,000 men. When trouble blew up with Boudica, he was hundreds of kilometres away.

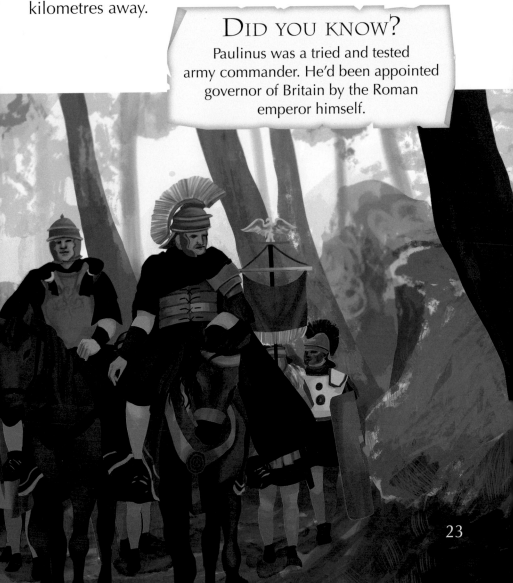

DID YOU KNOW?

Paulinus was a tried and tested army commander. He'd been appointed governor of Britain by the Roman emperor himself.

WHAT DID BOUDICA DO?

Around 60 CE, Boudica decided to form an army and drive the Romans out of Britain. She had fighters of her own, but she needed more. She talked to the leaders of the Trinovantes tribe, who lived near the Iceni.

Boudica told them what the Romans had done to her family and her tribe. She said that the Romans treated everyone badly. They'd stolen land from the Trinovantes and demanded high taxes from them too! Would the Trinovantes die as slaves, she asked, or stand up to the Romans? Boudica convinced the leaders. They agreed to join her army.

Boudica planned to raid Colchester. She knew Roman troops were in north Wales and that the capital was almost unguarded. She marched her army towards it.

DID YOU KNOW?

Some people believed there were bad **omens** in Colchester before Boudica's raid. It's said that a large statue smashed to the ground and the river turned blood red.

A CLOSER LOOK:
BOUDICA'S FIGHTERS

Boudica's army was made up of men, women and even children.

Warriors carried a long iron sword and a sharp spear for throwing.

Boudica's fighters rushed forwards into battle in a wild, noisy attack. They shouted loudly, and blew loud horns. It must have been terrifying for the enemy!

Warriors fought on foot, on horseback or in chariots. Chariots were quick and light.

Some people wore bronze helmets to protect the head. They sometimes had real horns on them, to make the fighter look fierce.

A long shield protected the body. Most shields were made from wood covered in leather. They were often decorated with circles and swirls.

27

WHAT HAPPENED AT COLCHESTER?

To the Romans in Colchester, Boudica's raid came out of the blue. Her **rebel** army marched in and set the town ablaze. Her fighters **ransacked** the burning houses and savagely killed everyone they found.

DID YOU KNOW?

Boudica's fighters smashed the gravestones of old Roman soldiers. You can see the cracked stones in Colchester today.

The local Roman soldiers were taken by surprise. They were completely outnumbered. Thousands of people fled to the temple for protection, but the rebel army surrounded and attacked it. After two days, the stone temple was destroyed along with everyone inside it.

Boudica must have enjoyed her revenge. Colchester, the capital of Roman Britain, was now a smoking ruin.

WHAT DID PAULINUS DO WHEN HE HEARD THE NEWS?

Paulinus was still in Wales. He and his army had crushed the Druids and were preparing to return home. When the Roman governor heard about the raid on Colchester, he was furious. How had this happened? He'd left the region in peace: now it was at war!

Paulinus thought long and hard: what would Boudica do next? He guessed that she'd attack London, an important Roman trading port. Could he possibly save it?

He had two **legions** of soldiers in Wales. He ordered the men to march back south while he quickly rode ahead with an advance guard.

DID YOU KNOW?

A legion is made up of 5,000 men. Paulinus had 10,000 soldiers in the wrong place at the wrong time.

a modern reconstruction showing what Paulinus's army might have looked like

WHAT HAPPENED IN LONDON?

When Paulinus arrived in London, he knew that he was too late. Boudica's army was on the march, and he had too few soldiers to fight it. He turned back round to meet his legions and left London to its fate.

Many Romans fled London. When Boudica's army arrived, her fighters destroyed and **looted** the town. They killed anyone who'd stayed behind. Then they marched on to St Albans, and in another brutal attack, they destroyed that town too.

Boudica was giddy with success. She knew Paulinus was gathering his soldiers, so she urged her fighters to march north and fight the Roman army.

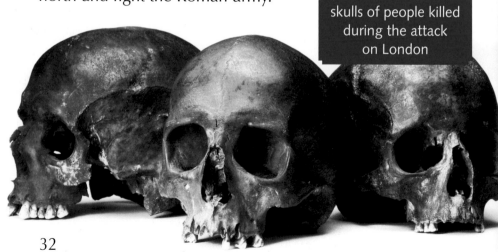

skulls of people killed during the attack on London

DID YOU KNOW?

There's a thick layer of burnt clay under the old Roman parts of London. This dates back to 60 CE, the time of Boudica's raid.

A CLOSER LOOK:
THE ROMAN ARMY

The Roman army was made up of small groups called "centuries". Each one contained 80 men and was led by a commander called a "centurion".

Centurions trained their men hard to keep them fit and strong. Centurions were very strict. Their soldiers obeyed them and did exactly what they said.

Roman soldiers wore good armour, made of metal scales. Underneath, they wore a linen shirt and a short woollen tunic.

DID YOU KNOW?
You didn't have to be born in Rome to serve as a soldier. Anyone in the Roman empire could join the army and become a citizen.

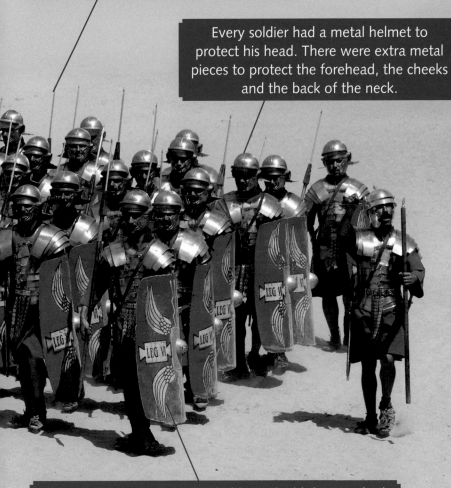

Roman soldiers carried long spears to throw at the enemy. They also had a short, light sword that was used for stabbing.

Every soldier had a metal helmet to protect his head. There were extra metal pieces to protect the forehead, the cheeks and the back of the neck.

Each soldier carried a curved oblong shield that reached from his chin to his knees. In the middle of the shield was a stud called a "boss". The soldier used this to push back the enemy or protect himself from blows.

HOW DID THE TWO ARMIES COMPARE?

When at last the two armies came face to face, they looked very different. We're told the Romans had 10,000 men but no one is really sure of the numbers. Their soldiers were well prepared for the battle. They lined up in tight rows and locked their shields together. This formed a solid wall that would be hard to break.

Boudica had about 200,000 men and women. They greatly outnumbered the enemy, but they were untrained, and only some of them wore armour.

For Boudica, the moment had come. She stood on a chariot and shouted to her troops, "On this field we must conquer or die!" Then she gave the signal to charge.

DID YOU KNOW?

Boudica's fighters were sure they'd win. They pulled their wagons into a ring so their families could watch the battle.

WHAT HAPPENED IN THE BATTLE?

Boudica's fighters rushed into battle. The Romans hurled their javelins at them, and many rebels were wounded. Boudica's army continued to attack, but the Romans held their ground.

These people are re-enacting a battle from Roman history.

After long hours of fighting, the rebels began to tire. The Romans then went on the attack. Their soldiers lined up in pointed wedges. These helped them to push into the enemy, and hack with their swords. The rebels panicked and tried to **retreat**, but they were trapped by their own wagons.

Nothing now could stop the Romans. Boudica's fighters died at their hands. The battle against Rome was lost.

DID YOU KNOW?

We're told that 80,000 of Boudica's fighters died in the battle, while the Romans only lost 400. We can't be sure of the true numbers.

HOW DID BOUDICA DIE?

We're not sure how Boudica died. One historian says she fell sick. Another tells us she killed herself with poison. Either way, Paulinus, the governor of Roman Britain, had his revenge on the rebels. The Iceni and Trinovantes were almost completely destroyed.

Paulinus had had a lucky escape. The Romans had almost lost control of Britain. The governor moved quickly to strengthen his power. He enlarged the Roman army and built extra forts.

News of the Iceni's defeat travelled like wildfire around the country. If other tribes had plans to rebel, this stopped them once and for all. There were no further rebellions, and Britain stayed in Roman hands for another 350 years.

HOW DO WE KNOW THE STORY OF BOUDICA?

Everything we know about Boudica was written by two historians. Cornelius Tacitus (55–120 CE) was a Roman historian. Cassius Dio (164–229 CE) was Greek. What they write is interesting, but we can't be sure it's true.

DID YOU KNOW?

Tacitus was only five years old when Boudica fought the Romans. Cassius Dio was born about 100 years after her death.

Over the centuries, Boudica has become a symbol of British courage. When Elizabeth I (1533–1603) was at war, she compared herself to the warrior queen. Later, in the 1850s, Queen Victoria approved a statue of Boudica. She said it would make people feel **patriotic**.

Boudica refused to become a slave. Her fighting spirit has been celebrated in books, films, paintings and stained glass. Her story is little more than **legend** yet it still lives on and inspires us today.

This picture of Boudica was painted by John Opie (1761–1807).

GLOSSARY

citizens	people who belonged to the Roman empire and had special rights
empire	a group of lands under the control of an emperor
famine	a shortage of food
Gaul	a country in Ancient Europe; now known as France
legend	an old story that may or may not be true
legions	parts of the Roman army; each legion contained about 5,000 soldiers
linen	a light cloth made from a plant called flax
looted	stole money during a raid
officials	people who hold a job and have power to control others
omens	signs of an event in the future
patriotic	having pride in your own country
ransacked	attacked and robbed a building
rebel	a person who resists his or her country's rulers
retreat	to move away from a fight and seek safety
taxes	payments made by ordinary people to the rulers of a country
trade	buying and selling
tribes	groups of people who live close together, and share the same language and way of life

INDEX

BOUDICA'S LIFE

Around 25 CE
Boudica is born.

43 CE
The Romans invade Britain.

20 CE   30 CE   40 CE

47 CE
King Prasutagus and Queen Boudica agree to work with the Romans. They stay on as rulers of the Iceni.

Around 59 CE

Paulinus takes his army to Wales to fight the Druids. King Prasutagus dies. His wealth and land are taken by the Romans. Boudica complains and is whipped. Her daughters are attacked.

50 CE   60 CE   70 CE

Around 60 CE

Boudica raises an army with the help of the Trinovantes. Her army attacks Colchester, London and St Albans.
In the final battle, Boudica's army fights the Romans.
The rebels are defeated.
Boudica dies.

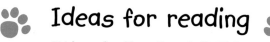

Ideas for reading

Written by Clare Dowdall, PhD
Lecturer and Primary Literacy Consultant

Reading objectives:
- retrieve and record information from non-fiction
- discuss their understanding and explain the meaning of words in context
- draw inferences and justify these with evidence

Spoken language objectives:
- participate in discussions, presentations, performances, role play, improvisations and debates

Curriculum links: History – The Roman Empire and its impact on Britain; Art and design – design, make, evaluate

Resources: Map of the UK showing Norfolk, ICT, materials for designing and building a model village

Build a context for reading
- Look at the front cover and share any knowledge that children have/suggest ideas about Boudica.
- Turn to the blurb. Read it aloud. Ask children to find the key words that give information about her, e.g. *warrior queen, leading into battle.*
- Ask children to behave like detectives. Look at the image on the back cover. What do they think the object is? What does it tell them?
- Create a spider diagram showing what's known about Boudica so far.

Understand and apply reading strategies
- Look at the contents together. Discuss how the book is organised.
- Turn to pp2–3. Ask children to read it quietly, looking for key information to add to the spider diagram. Discuss their findings and model how to retrieve and collect key information from reading.